THE DIGGERS ARE COMING!

Susan Steggall

F

FRANCES LINCOLN
CHILDREN'S BOOKS

For Ed

LONDON BOROUGH OF WANDSWORTH	
9030 00002 9246 7	
Askews & Holts	06-Dec-2012
JF	£11.99
	WWX0010293/0075

Text and illustrations copyright © Susan Steggall 2012
The right of Susan Steggall to be identified as the author and
illustrator of this work has been asserted by her in accordance with
the Copyright, Designs and Patents Act, 1988 (United Kingdom).

First published in Great Britain in 2012 and in the USA in 2013 by
Frances Lincoln Children's Books, 4 Torriano Mews,
Torriano Avenue, London NW5 2RZ
www.franceslincoln.com

A catalogue record for this book is available from the British Library.

ISBN 978-1-84780-288-0

Illustrated with collages of torn paper

Printed in Shenzhen, Guangdong, China by C&C Offset Printing in August 2012

135798642

They *shave*
and s h i f t
and **shove** all day,
scraping soil
and stones away.

The diggers are coming!
The diggers are coming,

with **MASSIVE** metal mouths.

Their teeth are tearing at the ground and their tracks trudge round and round and round

The tippers are coming!
The tippers are coming,

they're topped up to the brim.

They tremble along

and
trundle
about,

then tip up and slip

the
whole
load
out.

The mixers are coming!
The mixers are coming,

they tumble   and twist
                 and turn,

churning concrete round and round,
to dollop down into the ground.

The builders are coming!
The builders are coming,

with hard hats
and hammers and hods.

They're **biffing**
and **bashing**

The cranes are coming!
The cranes are coming,

with jibs and jacks
and booms.

They heave HUGE hefty hulks

up high and hold them hanging in the sky.

and steadily squash
all the bumpy bits out.

The vans are coming! The vans are coming,

with cupboards and chairs and chests.

They've *hurtled* halfway through the town.

They're stacked
with stuff,
but it's well strapped down.

The people are coming!
The people are coming,
with boxes and bundles and bags.

They`re moving in, and today`s the day!
Everything`s done and they`re here to stay.